# Riddles And Brain Teasers For Kids

*The Greatest Collection of Logic Riddles for Expanding Your Mind & Boosting Your Brain Power*

# Table of Contents

# Introduction

One of the most important elements of raising children is to make sure they are kept busy and well stimulated. It is crucial to keep your child's mind stimulated and active, to help them develop at an early age and increase their mental capabilities. This can be pretty difficult, as children tend to prefer playing around outside or watching television.

Luckily, riddles are a great solution for this problem. They are fun, entertaining, and suitable for all ages. Not only are they great for teaching your child how to think logically and outside-the-box, but they also help increase everyday brain activity.

This book is filled with riddles of all types. From short and easy one-line riddles, to brain teasers that might keep you guessing for a little longer. There are even a few riddles and games that are great for the whole family to enjoy together. This book is extremely easy to use. Each riddle is placed into a suitable category, making it easy to find and pick according to the mood. There are also solutions at the end of each riddle set. Hope you have fun learning and growing!

# Chapter 1: Short And Sweet

These are the simple riddles that are quick, short, and easy to understand. They are great to get young children started and introduce them to the wonderful world of riddles.

## What Am I?

1. No matter how far I go, I'm always at home. What am I?

2. I can be caught but not thrown. What am I?

3. I have a horn, and I bring milk, but I'm not a cow. What am I?

4. I can travel all over the world, but I always stay in the corner. What am I?

5. The more I dry, the more I get wet. What am I?

6. I have a head and a tail, and I can be flipped to make choices. What am I?

7. I'm not a bird or a bug, but I use my big wings to fly in the sky. What am I?

8. I have many keys, but I cannot be used to open a door. What am I?

9. I have a face and hands, but I can't smile or clap. What am I?

10. When I'm clean, I am black. When I'm dirty, I'm white. What am I?

11. I run all around the garden, but I never move a single inch. What am I?

12. I have a thin body and a small eye, and if you're not careful, I might make you cry. What am I?

13. You can find me in scarves, socks, and mittens, and I'm great fun for little kittens. What am I?

14. I go up and up, but I can never come down. What am I?

15. I have four legs, but I cannot walk. I am an important part of every meal, but I am not food. What am I?

# *Answers*

1. A turtle/snail

2. A cold

3. A milk truck

4. A postage stamp

5. A towel

6. A coin

7. An airplane

8. A piano

9. A clock

10. A chalkboard

11. A fence

12. A sewing needle

13. Yarn/wool

14. Age

15. A table

# What Is It?

1.  What becomes more the more you give it away?

2.  What has an ear that cannot hear?

3.  What is yours, even if others use it more than you do?

4.  What can you put in a box to make it lighter?

5.  Which letter in the alphabet is filled with water?

6.  The more you have of it, the less you can see. What is it?

7. What begins with a p, ends with an e, and has a million letters?

8. What runs but never walks?

9. You can hold it, but never touch it. What is it?

10. What has teeth, but cannot chew?

11. What can you always make, but never see?

12. What is broken as soon as you mention it?

13. What goes up when the rain falls down?

14. What can be as big as an elephant or a house, but will never weigh anything?

15. What becomes bigger the more you take away?

16. What has hundreds of needles, but never sews?

17. Which question can never be answered with "yes"?

# *Answers*

1. Love
2. A cup/mug.
3. Your name.
4. A hole.
5. C.
6. Darkness.
7. A post office.
8. A river.
9. Your breath.
10. A fork/comb
11. Noise.
12. Silence.
13. An umbrella
14. A shadow
15. A hole
16. A porcupine.
17. Are you asleep?

# Puns and Funny Riddles

1.  Why does Peter Pan always fly?

2.  Why can a pirate never finish the alphabet?

3.  Why did Mickey Mouse become an astronaut?

4.  Which tree can be carried in your hand?

5.  Why do bees always hum?

6.  Why do teddy bears never get hungry?

7.  Where do mermaids keep their money?

8.  What has rings, but no fingers?

9.  What type of cup can't be filled with water?

10. What type of room has no windows or doors?

11. Why did the teacher wear sunglasses to school?

12. What can you never eat for breakfast?

13. What do lazy dogs do for fun?

14. What can you pick, but never choose?

15. What tastes better than it smells?

# Answers

1. He Neverlands.

2. He always gets lost at "C" (sea).

3. He wanted to visit Pluto.

4. A palm.

5. They don't know the words to any songs.

6. They are always stuffed.

7. In a riverbank.

8. A telephone.

9. A cupcake.

10. A mushroom.

11. Her students were very bright.

12. Lunch and dinner.

13. They chase parked cars.

14. Your nose.

15. A tongue.

# Chapter 2: Right in the Middle

These are a little longer, and might be a little more difficult, but they are still fun, easy, and great for all ages.

## What Am I?

1. I can be found in many different colors and I sometimes smell nice. You can find me in the garden or buy me in a shop, and I'll stay pretty for longer if you give me water. What am I?

2. I'm round and bright, and I live in the sky, but you should never look at me. I go away at night but come back in the morning. What am I?

3. I fall down but never get hurt, and I can never go back up again. People go inside when I come, but children often want to play. What am I?

4. I go up and down, but never move out of place. What am I?

5. I have four thumbs and a finger, but no arm, hand, or bones. What am I?

6. I have a head and four legs, but only one foot. What am I?

7. My cover can be hard or soft. I have a spine but no bones, and I once was a tree. What am I?

8. I go off when I wake you, but I always stay in the same place. What am I?

9. I keep a boat from moving through the water, yet every boat has me. What am I?

10. People buy me to eat, but I am never eaten. What am I?

11. I lose my head in the morning, but I always get it back at night. I am often used for a safe, fun fight. What am I?

12. People always want me and always need me, but they're always giving me away. What am I?

13. I am long and thin, and I twist and turn. I can make a long loop that can help you when you walk. What am I?

14. I am not a tailor, but I have lots of clothes. I won't cry if you undress me, but you might. What am I?

15. I have a long neck and the name of a bird. I feed on cargo ships, yet I am not alive. What am I?

16. I am wood, but I am not hard. I am neither straight nor crooked. What am I?

17. I am black when you buy me, and red when you use me. But when you are done, I am grey and white. What am I?

# *Answers*

1. A flower.

2. The Sun.

3. Rain/snow.

4. Stairs.

5. A glove.

6. A bed.

7. A book.

8. An alarm.

9. An anchor.

10. A plate.

11. A pillow.

12. Money.

13. A shoestring.

14. An onion.

15. A crane.

16. Sawdust.

17. Charcoal.

# How and What?

1. What can fill a room in an instant, yet take up no space at all?

2. What is always close behind you, but you will never see it again?

3. How can a pocket be completely empty, yet still have something in it?

4. The more you take, the more you leave behind. What are they?

5. What needs to be answered, yet never asks any questions?

6. It sparkles and is white, it goes down but never up, and children like to make angels with it. What is it?

7. What is always coming, but never arrives?

8. What is full of holes, yet still holds water?

9. If you have it, you want to share it, but if you share it, you no longer have it. What is it?

10. What looks like a cat, sounds like a cat, and acts like a cat, but isn't a cat?

11. What goes through towns and over mountains all day and all night, but never moves?

12. What can you use to see through a wall?

# *Answers*

1. Light.

2. Yesterday.

3. The pocket has a hole in it.

4. Footsteps.

5. A doorbell.

6. Snow.

7. Tomorrow

8. A sponge.

9. A secret.

10. A kitten.

11. A road.

12. A window.

# _A Short message from the Author_:

Hey, are you enjoying the book? I'd love to hear your thoughts!

Many readers do not know how hard reviews are to come by, and how much they help an author.

I would be incredibly grateful if you could take just 60 seconds to write a brief review on Amazon, even if it's just a few sentences!

Thank you for taking the time to share your thoughts!

Your review will genuinely make a difference for me and help gain exposure for my work.

# With a Twist

1. A man drives to a building with three doors, One gold, one silver, and one lead. Which door does he open first?

2. How many seconds are there in a year?

3. Where can you find Friday before Thursday?

4. There are seven months in the year that have 31 days. How many months have 28 days?

5. When the bus leaves town, there are 12 people on it. When it stops at the next town, two people get on and five get off. It stops again and three people get on. At the next stop, three people get off and five get on. At the next, seven get off and none get on. At

the next stop, 10 get on and 11 get off. At the last stop no one gets off and one person gets on. How many times did the bus stop?

6. Milly's mother has five daughters. Her first four are called Lala, Lele, Lili, and Lolo. What is her fifth daughter called?

7. What is the very last thing you always take off before going to bed?

8. Which word is always spelled wrong in every single dictionary?

9. What do you call someone who doesn't have all his fingers on one hand?

10. How many sides does a circle have?

11. A butcher is six feet tall, he wears size nine shoes, and has a wife and a daughter. What does he weigh?

12. A boy fell off a very tall ladder, but why didn't he get hurt at all?

13. A farmer has eight chickens, four pigs, and seven cows. If we call the cows pigs, how many pigs will he have.

14. If it takes three men a day to dig a hole, how long will it take two men to dig half a hole?

15. You are driving a bus with seven people on board and stop at your hometown. One person gets off, three get on. Then six more people get off, and then five get on. Two people get on, and one gets off. What color are the driver's eyes?

16. How can you make seven even?

17. The word has six letters, and when you remove one it is twelve. What is the word?

18. It starts with T, ends with T, and has T in it. What is it?

19. How can you make the number one disappear?

20. Why is the letter T like an island?

21. A blue house is made out of blue bricks, a red house is made of red bricks, and a yellow house is made out of yellow bricks. What is a greenhouse made out of?

22. In a small, one story building, the walls are pink, the doors are pink, the furniture is pink,

the window frames are pink, and the roof is pink. What color are the stairs?

23. In a large, round house, the owner finds a grape juice stain on the carpet. To find out who was responsible, he asked everyone what they were doing that morning. "I was playing outside," said his son. "I was sitting in the corner, reading," said his daughter. "I was making lunch," said his wife. Who was lying?

24. Somebody left through the front door. Nobody left through the back door. Who is in the house?

25. It happens once in a lifetime, twice a moment, a minute, but never in a hundred years. What is it?

26. Two is company, three is a crowd. What are four and five?

27. How far can a fox run into the forest?

28. What five letter word becomes shorter by adding two letters?

29. Mary has four daughters. Each of her daughters have a brother. How many children does Mary have?

# *Answers*

1. His car door.

2. 2nd January, 2nd February, 2nd March, etc.

3. In a dictionary.

4. All twelve months have at least 28 days in them.

5. The bus stopped six times.

6. Her name is Milly, not Lulu—which might have been your first thought.

7. You take your feet off the floor.

8. The word "wrong".

9. Normal, he should have five fingers on both hands, not 10 on one.

10. Two. The inside and the outside.

11. He weighs meat.

12. He was standing on the first step of the ladder.

13. He will still have 4 pigs. Calling the cows pigs doesn't mean they're not cows.

14. You cannot dig just half a hole.

15. The color of the driver's eyes depends on your own eyes, as you are the driver.

16. Remove the letter s and the word seven becomes the word even.

17. Dozens.

18. A teapot.

19. Add the letter *g* and it will be *gone*.

20. It is in the middle of water.

21. Glass.

22. There are no stairs, since the house doesn't have a second story.

23. Ton.

24. This isn't a question. It is a statement. Somebody, Nobody, and Who are the names of people.

25. The letter *m*.

26. Nine.

27. Halfway. After that it starts running out of the forest again.

28. Short.

29. Five, as all four sisters share the same brother.

# Chapter 3: Challenge Yourself

This chapter is for those who are looking for more of a challenge, as they require a little more thinking work. These may be a little difficult for very small children, but they are great for those a little older who have already developed beyond the level of the super easy stuff.

## What Am I?

1. Small and pretty am I. I have delicate wings with which I fly. Flowers are my food but honey I do not make. What am I?

2. I have a tail that is long and a coat that is brown. I love the country, the city, and the town. I can live in a house or live in a shed,

and I come out to play when the cat goes to bed. What am I?

3. I have two sides, but only one can be used. I can be held in your hand or hung on a wall. I will always tell you the truth, though I say nothing at all. What am I?

4. I am the end of time and space, the beginning of the end. I am the center of creation and I surround every place. What am I?

5. My father is a cloud, my mother is the wind. My son is the river, my daughter is the plants on the land. My crown is a rainbow and my grave is the ground. I can be both a blessing and a curse to man. What am I?

6. You throw away my outside and cook my inside. Then you eat my outside and throw away my inside. What am I?

7. I can be born in silence, but usually not. I am never seen, but you immediately know I'm there. I do no harm, yet nobody wants me there. What am I?

8. I have a heart that doesn't beat, and a home where I never sleep. I can build my own house and take another's. Although I rule, I play games with my brothers. I have a wife and a son, and ten loyal servants. What am I?

9. I have a head but do not weep, I have a bed but do not sleep. I have a mouth that cannot speak, and an eye that cannot seek. I am poor but have a bank. What am I?

10. I am a food and a seed with only three letters to my name. Take away two, and I still sound the same. What am I?

11. I can be cracked or played, told, or made. I am born in your head, but I have to be said. What am I?

12. I go in dry and come out wet. The longer I stay the stronger I get. What am I?

13. I am food with five letters but remove the first and I become energy. Remove another letter, and you'll need me to live. Mix up those three letters, and I become a nice drink. What am I?

14. We come out at night without being called and disappear in the morning without being stolen. What are we?

# *Answers*

1. A butterfly.

2. A mouse.

3. A mirror.

4. The letter *e*.

5. A river.

6. A cob of corn.

7. A fart.

8. The King of Hearts.

9. A river.

10. A pea.

11. A joke.

12. A teabag.

13. Wheat.

14. Stars.

# How and What?

1. It has roots that nobody sees and is taller than trees. Up, up it goes, but never it grows. What is it?

2. Black and furry, it flies around. Try not to be scared if you can. It sleeps in a cave and hangs upside down. For a superhero, just put it before man. What is it?

3. What has keys that cannot lock a door, space but not a room, and can enter, but never go outside?

4. You can see it, you can smell it, but you cannot touch it. It has no hands, no feet, and no wings, but still it climbs into the sky. What is it?

5. Which question can you ask all day long, receive a different answer every time, and yet the answers will still always be right?

6. Five siblings need to sit in a row of five chairs. Billy and Bobby always fight, so they can never sit together. Milly is angry at Sarah, so they can't sit together either, while Sarah is angry at Billy. Tom doesn't like his sisters, so he'll need to sit with his brothers. In which order would you arrange the children to make them happy?

7. What word will always be right if it is pronounced wrong, but will be wrong if pronounced right?

8. What starts out tall, but becomes shorter as the night grows longer?

9. You hear it shout through the streets, though it has no voice and no lung. It plays with the leaves and throws them at people both old and young. What is it?

10. It doesn't matter if you use it a lot or only a little, every month you need to change it. What is it?

11. What has two arms but no hands, and a neck but no head?

12. It can't be seen, felt, heard, or smelt. It lies behind stars, under hills, and empty holes it fills. It comes first and follows after. It takes life and kills laughter. What is it?

13. What walks on four legs in the morning, on two legs at noon, and three legs in the evening.

# *Answers*

1.  A mountain.

2.  A cat.

3.  A keyboard.

4.  Smoke.

5.  What time is it?

6.  Milly, Billy, Tom, Bobby, and Sarah.

7.  Wrong.

8.  A candle.

9.  The wind.

10. A calendar.

11. A shirt.

12. Darkness.

13. Mankind. A human crawls when it is a baby, walks on two legs when it grows up, and uses a cane when it gets old.

# How Is It Possible?

1. A man walks outside in the rain with no coat, hat, or umbrella, but his hair never gets wet. How is this possible?

2. There are six apples in a basket and six children. Each child gets an apple, but there's still one apple in the basket. How is this possible?

3. Two mothers and two daughters go out to dinner. Each one eats a hamburger, and in total three hamburgers were eaten. How is this possible?

4. A cowboy rides into town on Friday. He stays in town for three days and leaves on Friday. How is this possible?

5. A horse is tied to a rope five meters long and its food is 15 meters away, but it still manages to reach the food. How is this possible?

6. A boy throws a ball as hard as he can. The ball doesn't bounce and no one else touches the ball, but it comes right back to the boy. How is this possible?

7. A man shaves several times every day, but he always goes to bed with a beard. How is this possible?

8. You see a boat filled with people, but there isn't a single person on board. How is this possible?

9. A boy stands one side of the river and his dog on the other. When the boy calls his dog, it crosses the river without using a bridge or

a boat, but it doesn't swim either and it doesn't get wet. How is this possible?

# *Answers*

1. He doesn't have any hair.

2. One of the children was given the basket with the apple in it.

3. They were a grandmother, a mother, and a daughter. The mother is a daughter as well.

4. The cowboy's horse is called Friday.

5. The other end of the rope isn't tied to anything.

6. The boy threw the ball straight up into the air.

7. He is a barber.

8. All the people on the boat are in a relationship.

9. The river is frozen, and the dog simply runs over the ice.

# Chapter 4: Family Fun

These are the games and riddles that the whole family can enjoy together.

## The Minister's Cat

This game is great for improving your vocabulary and is great for large crowds. Both children and adults can play this, and it is a great way for very small children to learn the alphabet. There are two ways to play the game, and two different ways to see who wins. The game tends to be more fun with larger groups.

To play, have everyone seated in a circle and the group chooses someone to start. That person then chooses a descriptive word starting with the letter *a*, such as angry, and says, "The minister's cat is an angry cat." The person next to them has to choose another descriptive *a* word, such as awesome, and says, "The minister's cat is an awesome cat." Keep going around until someone either chooses a word that has already been used or cannot think of a descriptive word starting with the letter *a* within ten seconds. That person either falls out of the game completely or gets one point. The next person starts up the game with words starting with the letter *b*. Keep playing the game, moving through the alphabet until there is only one player left or until you've played through the entire alphabet. If you're using the system of falling out, the last player still in the game wins. If you're using a point system, the winner is the player with the least points at the end of the game.

For an easier, potentially shorter version of the game, rather than keeping with the same letter until someone falls out or gets a point, the first player chooses an *a* letter, the second player chooses a *b* letter, the third player chooses a *c* letter, and so on. Once everyone has had a turn, the first player goes on to the next letter. For example, if there are five players, the fifth player uses the letter *e*, so the first player has to use the letter *f.* Anyone who can't think of a word with their letter falls out of the game. This version might be better for smaller children, but it may be necessary to go through the alphabet a few times to find a winner. If that is the case, no words from previous rounds can be used.

# Repeat After Me

This is a game great for improving memory and can be thought of as a vocal group version of memory tiles. This is another game well suited for both adults and children but works better with slightly smaller groups.

Once again, have everyone sit in a circle and choose a player to start. The starting player says any two random words that come to mind. The next player has to repeat the first two words and add their own two words. The third player has to repeat those four words and once again add his own two words. An example of a typical word chain can be something like, "Yes, today, apple, blue, shirt, hippo, bacon, never" etc. This is after four players have had their turn. Keep repeating and adding words until a player gets the order wrong or forgets one of the words. That player falls out of the game and the game starts with two new words. The last player remaining wins the game. As a bonus goal for the game: Try to build the word chain as long as possible.

For a simpler version that might be better suited for younger children, limit the usable words to specific subjects, such as using only colors, numbers, animals, etc. As your children grow older, you can use two subjects, then three, and so on, that there aren't any specific subjects anymore. Or you can limit it to one syllable words, then add two syllable words, etc. The rules of this game can be altered to let it develop together with your children. For teens and adults, it can be fun to try and use as strange and obscure words as possible for an extra challenge.

In this game, it doesn't matter if you use the same word more than once, but you can make it a rule if you want to use this game to improve vocabulary, though it will be more effective if you keep the words limited to specific subjects.

# Beginning With the End

This is a word game that is great for improving vocabulary, memory skills, and working on spelling. Initially, this game is meant for two players, but it can be played with more players as well.

The first player once again chooses a word once again. The second player then needs to choose a word that starts with the letter the previous word ends with. The first player then has to give another word that once again starts with the same letter that the previous word ended with. Here's an example of a few rounds of the game: laptop, potato, octopus, salad, dance, evil, lean, now, wonder. The game ends when a player repeats a previously used word or can't think of a suitable word within ten seconds of their turn starting. If you are playing with more than two players, you can sit in a circle and go either clockwise or counter clockwise, with any losing players falling out of the game until there's only one player remains.

For this game, you can't use names, places, or words from a foreign language. The game may take very long, and you may get tired of it before a winner can be determined. To make it a bit more of a challenge, you can limit the subject or number of syllables of the words you can use. You can also decrease the amount of time the players have to give an answer or you can set the rules that the players have to start their word with the last two letters of the previous word, e.g. life, feel, elevate, team, amble, lesson, onion, only.

# Once upon a Time and Tell My Story

Here are two games that may not be considered riddles or brain teasers, but can be used to help develop creativity, strengthen improvisation skills, and improve visual communication.

The first game, once upon a time, is for multiple players, It doesn't have a winner or a loser, and ends whenever the players want it to. To start the game, the players must sit in a circle. The first player starts with, "Once upon a time," and completes the sentence however they want, e.g., "Once upon a time there lived a giant dragon." Working either clockwise or counter clockwise, the next player adds their own sentence to continue the story, e.g., "This dragon was sad, because he was much smaller than all the other dragons." Each player adds a new sentence to the story. The aim of the game is to create a new story that is as entertaining, funny, and outlandish as possible while still making sense. You may want to have someone who isn't a player write down the story as it progresses and read it back to the players once it is done.

Tell My Story is a game for two players, but it can be played in groups, where the winners of each group play against each other. The first player tries to tell a simple story using only gestures and available objects but isn't allowed to use words, trying to make the gestures as clear as possible. The second player interprets the story the player wants to tell and has to try to tell a different story that still matches the gestures but doesn't match the story the first player is trying to tell. As an example, the first player gestures going onto one knee and opening a small box for the other player. The obvious story is that the player is proposing. The second player then says that the first player has injured his leg and fell to his knee and is opening a box with an emergency button in it.

In the next round, the player must tell a story with gestures that matches the story that the second player has told. Once again, the second player needs to interpret the story and try to tell a different story. This story also has to match the story the second player started to tell in the previous round. This game can be played in three or four rounds.

There are two ways to win the game. If you are the first player, you win the game by using gestures to force the second player to tell the story you want. If you are the second player you win the game by telling a story that makes sense, works with the gestures, and is very clearly not the story the first player was trying to tell.

# *The End... Almost!*

Reviews are not easy to come by.

As an independent author with a tiny marketing budget, I rely on readers, like you, to leave a short review on Amazon.

Even if it's just a sentence or two!

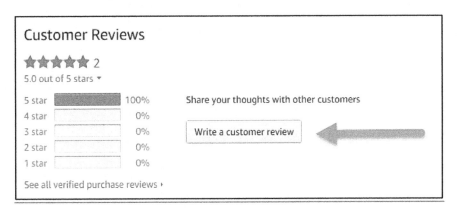

So, if you enjoyed the book, please leave a brief review on Amazon.

I am very appreciative for your review as it truly makes a difference.

Thank you from the bottom of my heart for purchasing this book and reading it to the end.

# Conclusion

Hopefully this book has helped you discover that learning, improving your logic, and raising your IQ doesn't need to be boring or difficult — it can be fun and entertaining!

Thank you for buying this book and taking the time to try out the riddles and brain teasers. Share them with others and have fun!

# References

101 Riddles That Will Stump You Every Time (But Don't Worry—We'll Give You the Answers). (2019). Retrieved from https://parade.com/947956/parade/riddles/

221 What am I Riddles and Answers for Kids. (2019). Retrieved from https://kidactivities.net/what-am-i-riddles-and-answers-for-kids/

Fun Easy Riddles For Kids With Answers. (n.d.). Retrieved from http://laffgaff.com/easy-riddles-for-kids-with-answers/

Kids Riddles. (n.d.). Retrieved from
https://www.riddles.com/kids-
riddles?page=1.Medium

Riddles. (n.d.). Retrieved from
https://www.riddles.com/medium-
riddles?page=1.Parade


These 33 Riddles are Perfect For Your Kid's Brain
Development. (2019). Retrieved from
https://www.fatherly.com/play/the-best-riddles-for-
kids-not-confusing/


Zhu, J., Neib, D., Kelly, N.W., Krishbopbopolis, U.,
Elz, & Reuben. (2019). 203 Fun Riddles for Kids
with Answers. Retrieved from
https://icebreakerideas.com/riddles-for-kids/